1/6/2012

MW01596535

Bless the Lord
the Alesun your then
Psalm 20:4

Sincerely
David Hoffins

Thanks for all
you do for
my boys.

Hope for Heavy Hearts

Surviving Life's Trials

David A. Paszkiewicz

authorHOUSE®

AuthorHouse™
1663 Liberty Drive, Suite 200
Bloomington, IN 47403
www.authorhouse.com
Phone: 1-800-839-8640

First published by AuthorHouse   3/19/2009

ISBN: 978-1-4389-3493-8 (sc)

Library of Congress Control Number: 2009900768

Printed in the United States of America
Bloomington, Indiana

This book is printed on acid-free paper.

This book is dedicated to the memory of Debra Lou.

It is also dedicated to those seeking true hope in the midst of impossible circumstances.

"May he give you the desire of your heart and make all your plans succeed."
Psalm 20:4

Preface

Hope for Heavy Hearts was born out of seven years of intense spiritual trial in my personal life. The principles in the book are those which carried me through and gave me hope. I have no doubt that they will offer you hope as well. The work is a collection of 12 short, inspiring essays rooted in biblical truth as well as the real world. The chapters can be read in order or in order of preference and are not meant to be exhaustive expositions of theological truth, but short, readable essays intended to offer immediate hope and encouragement to the reader.

My Prayer for the Reader

"May He give you the desire of your heart and make all your plans succeed." Psalm 20:4

God's Word to the Reader

"For I know the plans I have for you," declares the Lord, "plans to prosper you and not to harm you, plans to give you hope and a future." Jeremiah 29:11

.

Contents

Chapter 1
Purpose in Pain

"Consider it pure joy, my brothers, whenever you face trials of many kinds, because you know that the testing of your faith develops perseverance. Perseverance must finish its work so that you may be mature and complete, not lacking anything." James 1:2-4

Sometimes it's hard to understand why God allows suffering, but you can be certain that He has a purpose in your pain.

A number of years ago, my sister, whom I dearly loved, went to her doctor with what she believed was a cough due to chest congestion. The doctor prescribed cough medicine and she thought nothing of it. Life went on as usual for a few weeks apart from the persistent cough. When she went back to the doctor, he ordered a chest x-ray. My family was devastated to learn she had stage four lung cancer. Debra Lou was only 47 and she had been vibrant, beautiful and fun loving. We were very close and I could not imagine my life without her. I never questioned God but I begged Him to heal her. I knew that God could do the impossible (Luke 1:37) and had hope that He would. However, as time went on and Debra's condition continued to deteriorate, we realized God had chosen not to heal her.

In hindsight, I can see God's purpose in all the pain. Debra's disease brought her closer to God. She confided in me that she knew she was going to die. She remembered asking Christ to be her Savior as a child but needed assurance from God's Word that she truly did belong to Him. She had led a rebellious life and never really served Him and she was fearful that God might forsake her. I assured her from the Scriptures that because her faith was solely in Jesus for her salvation, she was in fact a child of God and did not need to fear separation from Him in death (John 3:16).

Debra suffered severe headaches as the cancer in her lungs spread to her brain. She suffered nausea from chemotherapy and lost her beautiful hair as a result of radiation treatments. In all her suffering, she never blamed God. Her preoccupation was with her loving husband Rick and her dying wish was to have assurance that he would meet her one day in Heaven. He was very religious but didn't have a personal relationship with Jesus Christ. She invited me to her house where I was able to pray with Rick as He invited Christ into his life. Debra's Bambi-like eyes filled with tears of joy.

Debra wanted her death to count for something and I was honored when she asked me to preach her funeral. She told me she didn't want just anyone preaching her funeral. She wanted a pastor whom she knew would preach the Gospel. Death is an inescapable reality for all of us. She wanted her friends and loved ones to be confronted with their own mortality so they might turn to Christ for Salvation (Hebrews 9:27).

Between her wake and funeral, I was able to preach three evangelistic sermons and I am certain God used her testimony to impact hearts. I know that souls turned to Christ and that Debra will see friends in Heaven one day as a result.

My family and I were with Debra every night for the last 30 days of her life. Those days were painful yet joyful at the same time. It was painful to see someone so precious wither away to nothing; nevertheless, in those 30 days nothing was left unsaid. Debra knew she was loved. I also had the privilege of gathering friends, loved ones and visitors around her for prayer and encouragement each night from God's Word. They needed it more than her. She seemed to be enveloped by God's peace.

As painful as the whole ordeal was, there was a Divine purpose in all the suffering. Debra grew close to God, our family drew closer together, her husband trusted Christ as Savior and others did as well at the funeral.

As for me, Debra's sickness and death were the beginning of what seemed to be a tsunami of spiritual trials for the next five years. My church experienced a painful division, my youngest daughter, Hannah, was diagnosed with a dangerous Kidney disease and I became the subject of a media firestorm over a church/state issue. Even today, I am not out of the furnace. My trials continue. However, I face them with peace and joy in my heart because I know that God has a purpose in my pain. If you are going through a trial my friend, you have that same assurance. God has a purpose for your pain. A. W. Tozer once said, "It is doubtful whether God can bless a man greatly until He has hurt him deeply."[1] If you are suffering, take heart and look forward with great expectation to being used and blessed by God.

Thoughts for today's meditation:
- There is purpose in your pain.
- Trials test your faith and build perseverance.
- You are going to be used by God.

Personal Reflections

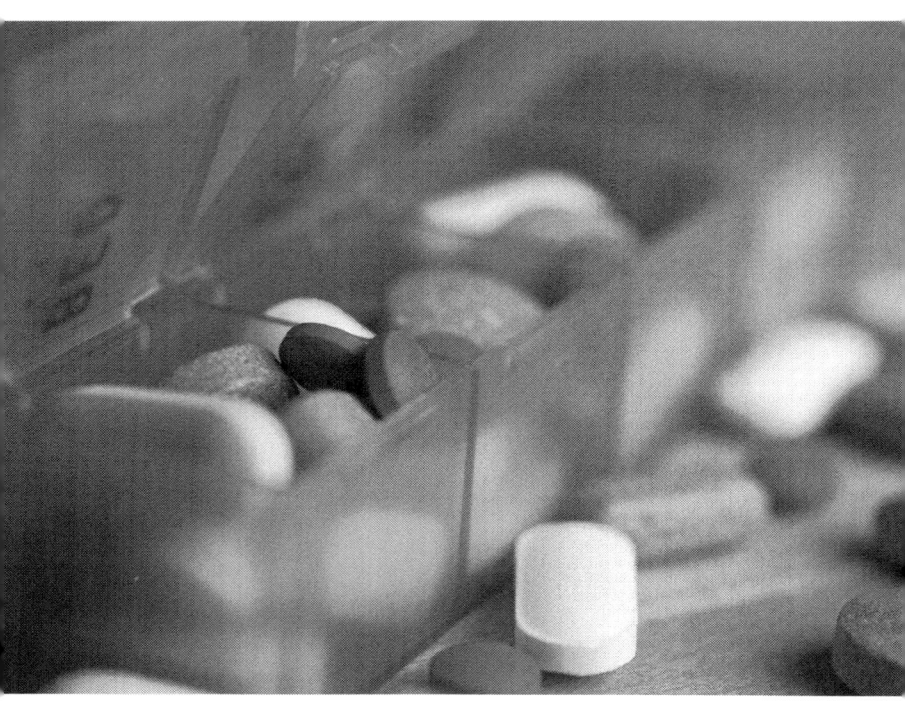

Chapter 2
A Prescription for Peace

"Do not be anxious about anything, but in everything, by prayer and petition, with thanksgiving, present your requests to God. And the peace of God, which transcends all understanding, will guard your hearts and minds in Christ Jesus." Philippians 4:6-7

Many believers have peace with God but never go on to experience the peace of God in their lives. They are troubled with anxieties and fears which rob them of peace and joy. This is unfortunate because inner peace is a gift of God and is available to all believers. It broke my heart to learn recently that the most frequently prescribed drugs in America are antidepressants. This is a tragedy. Americans spend millions of dollars medicating their unhappiness and lasting peace eludes them. It doesn't have to be this way.

The Bible teaches that the believer in Jesus Christ is indwelled by the Holy Spirit of God (John 14:16-17, 27). When an individual trusts Christ as Savior the Holy Spirit actually takes up residence inside of him. This is an incredible truth. The Creator of the universe literally resides in the individual. Think of the power you have access to as a child of God! Does He hear your prayers? Of course He does; He lives inside of you! He not only hears your prayers but He is acutely aware of every anxious thought and He cares (I Peter 5:7)!

Believers are actually commanded to be "filled" or controlled by the Holy Spirit. Ephesians 5:18 states: *"Do not get drunk on wine, which leads to debauchery. Instead, be filled with the Spirit."* As you read this verse you might wonder, what in the world do wine and the Holy Spirit have in common? There are two ways of looking at it and I believe both are correct. First, wine is a controlling agent. The drunkard is controlled, in a sense, by his desire for the wine. Instead of being controlled by wine or the sinful nature, be controlled by the Holy Spirit of God who lives inside of you. The second way of looking at it is that wine lifts an individual's inhibitions. A drunken man does things he would never do when he is sober. Likewise, the Holy Spirit lifts those inhibitions which keep us from doing good. With these inhibitions lifted, we are able to serve God freely. Why is this important for you? Well if you seek the peace of God in your heart, the Bible says that the Holy Spirit is the source of peace (John 14:26-27). Inner peace is a "fruit" of the Holy Spirit in the life of the believer (Galatians 5:22). If one has trusted Christ as Savior, He has the Holy Spirit. If one has the Holy Spirit and he allows him to control him, peace will fill his heart. An important part of the process is allowing the Spirit to control your mind. This is done by regenerating your thoughts through filling your mind with those things that are virtuous (Romans 8:6-8 and Philippians 4:8). Our minds are like computers. If you program junk into a computer, that is exactly what you get out of it. Likewise, if you fill your mind with junk, that's exactly what will emanate from your life.

Why do so many of us lack inner peace? First of all, lack of peace stems from worry. There are essentially only two things we worry about in life: 1. those things we **can** do something about and 2. those things we **can't** do anything about. If that which occupies your thoughts and keeps you up at night is in the first category, do something about it! Perhaps you have sinned against someone. Perhaps you treated someone unfairly. Don't delay. The thing to do is confess and apologize. If the individual forgives you great! If not, they are sinning by holding a grudge. Nevertheless, you can have full assurance that God has forgiven you and that is what matters most (I John 1:9). If what you are worrying about is in the second category, why worry? There is **nothing** you can do; put it in God's hands (I Peter 5:7). You are His child and He will carry the burden for you!

So what is God's prescription for inner peace? It's found in Philippians 4:6-7, *"Do not be anxious about anything, but in everything, by prayer and petition, with thanksgiving, present your requests to God. And the peace of God, which transcends all understanding, will guard your hearts and your minds in Christ Jesus."* God says:

1. Be prayerful in everything. (Philippians 4:6)
2. Be thankful for anything. (Philippians 4:6)
3. And you will have peace! (Philippians 4:7)

Today, my friend, put your anxious thoughts at ease by following the above prescription. Remember whose child you are if you belong to Christ. Remember that the Holy Spirit of God dwells inside of you and that He is the source of real peace. Follow God's prescription in Philippians 4:6-7 and get the rest your weary soul needs.

Perhaps you read the above and you desire the inner peace of God but you don't have peace with God. This is the most important decision you can make. Put your faith and trust in Jesus Christ and you will be a child of God (John 1:12-13). Why not confess your need of a Savior to Him in prayer and ask Him to forgive you of your sins and be your Savior (see appendix 1)? The promise is that He will! This is the first step in accessing God's peace.

Thoughts for today's meditation:

- Inner peace comes from the Holy Spirit.
- If one has the Holy Spirit, and allows Him to control him, peace will fill his heart.
- Be prayerful and thankful in all circumstances and you will have peace.

Personal Reflections

Chapter 3
Overcoming the Impossible

"For nothing is impossible with God." Luke 1:37

Have you ever been in an impossible situation? Were you ever boxed in on all sides by the circumstances of life with no way out? You are not alone. The children of Israel faced a similar crisis when Moses led them out of Egyptian bondage. The story is recounted in Exodus chapter 14. After 430 years in slavery to the Egyptians, it appeared God finally delivered them. Nevertheless, in a short time, they found themselves facing the Red Sea, hemmed in by dessert on their right and left, with well over six hundred chariots speeding toward them from behind. The Israelites trusted God for their deliverance but it seemed He actually led them to their doom. Their situation was impossible. They were unarmed, with women and children, and they had nowhere to flee. The Bible says, *"They were terrified and cried out to the Lord."* (Exodus 14:10b). Moses' response was, *"... Do not be afraid. Stand firm and you will see the deliverance the Lord will bring you today ... The Lord will fight for you; you need only to be still."* (Exodus 14:13,14). The Israelite's situation was impossible, yet you know the rest of the story. God parted the Red Sea and provided a way of escape! The Israelites escaped on dry ground but the sea swallowed Pharaoh's army. Nothing is impossible for God! (Luke 1:37).

There are a number of encouraging principles, which can be drawn from this episode of Israel's History that can be applied to our lives. First, when you are in an "impossible" situation, take comfort in knowing that God is aware of your crisis. In the case of the Israelites, God actually gave them specific directions that led them into their impossible situation. He told them to camp against the Red sea! (Exodus 14:2). The Israelites didn't understand it right away, but God was creating circumstances, which would enable Him to reveal His power and strengthen their faith (Exodus 14:31). Perhaps God is doing the same in your life. Second, know that there are no mistakes in God's economy. To the child of God there is no such thing as an accident or coincidence (Proverbs 16:4,9,33). God is in control! You are not in your situation by accident; God has a plan! Third, pray. God delivered the Israelites in direct response to prayer (Exodus 14:10). Fourth, be patient. In Exodus 14:14 Moses said, *"The Lord will fight for you; you need only to be still."* While in crisis, the tendency is to try to escape via the path of least resistance. No one likes pain and trials hurt. Avoid this tendency; Exercise faith and wait on God. Psalm 46:10a says, *"Be still and know that I am God..."* When in an impossible situation, be still and get out of God's way! Trust Him to deliver you. He will not let you down. Thinking about the following attributes of God will bring you hope:

1. God is omnipresent; He is everywhere and He knows your situation!
2. God is omnipotent: there is no problem too big for Him!

3. God is omniscient; no problem is too difficult to solve!
4. God is immutable; He does not change (James 1:17)! The God who delivered the children of Israel can and will enter the impossible situation you are facing and part the Red Sea you are up against if you trust Him! Will you?

Thoughts for today's meditation:

- For the believer, there is no such thing as an accident or coincidence.
- You are not in your situation by accident; God has a plan!
- Exercise faith and wait on God.

Personal Reflections

Personal Reflections

Chapter 4
Miracles are Rare but God's Providences are not!

"And we know in all things God works for the good of those who love him, who have been called according to his purpose." Romans 8:28

People crave the miraculous. When it comes to the church, you can actually boost attendance by promising healing and miracle services. However, **miracles are rare.** By definition, a miracle is a supernatural event which is contrary to the laws of nature. An example would be Jesus' turning water to wine, walking on the water, or raising Lazarus from the dead. Such incredible events in history are inspiring. Yet, the fact that they are rare events can be a source of discouragement to the believer in crisis looking for hope. However, do not despair! I am not writing this to take away your hope, but to increase it! **Although miracles are rare, God's providences are not!**

God's providence is his loving care over His creation through natural processes. Remember, God is the creator of the natural order, therefore He is certainly capable of using the laws of nature to bring about His will in the circumstances of the believer. The Bible says, *"The Lord works out everything for his own ends..."* (Proverbs 16:4a). It also states. *"And we know in all things God works for the good of those who love him,..."* (Romans 8:28:a). Imagine that! In all *"things"*

God works for the good of those who love Him! I am struck by the word *"things"* in this passage. Do you know what *"things"* this verse speaks of? The *"things"* are the circumstances that the believer finds himself in. God cares about your circumstances and He is working them out for your good! What a wonderful promise! If you are in a crisis, if you are in what seems to be an impossible or unbearable situation, maintain hope! God promises He is working things out for your good. In addition, you can be certain that God has the power to alter the circumstances you find yourself in.

A number of years ago I found myself in the middle of a crisis of faith. As a high school crew coach I was determined to honor God by not racing on Sundays. One concession I made to the school was the State Championship Regatta. It was on Sunday and I felt that it would be unfair to the students if I prevented them from racing because of my convictions. After all, it was a public school and the students in general did not share my convictions. This particular season, the athletic director put pressure on me to race an additional Sunday. I was the girls' varsity coach and the boys' team had scheduled an additional Sunday race. It would double our expenses if I took the girls to a Saturday race while the boys' team raced on Sunday because we shared the same boat trailer. It was clear the athletic director expected me to be a "team" player and race in the Sunday regatta along with the boys' team. My response to him was that my convictions were that there should be no racing on Sundays and that I was already compromising my standards by having the team race in the State Championship Regatta. I told him that perhaps it was time to consider looking for a coach more inclined to agree with racing on Sundays. He asked me to reconsider but fully expected me to fulfill my obligation to the team and do the Sunday race. I told him I would but that I was also going to pray for the race to be cancelled. To make a long story short, I prayed for the race to be cancelled so that I could be back in time to be in the Sunday morning service at my church. It was the second week of April in Kearny New Jersey. We left our boathouse parking lot at 6:30am and were only on the road for 30 minutes when we were hit by a blinding snowstorm! The bus actually had to turn around because visibility was so poor. In short, we were back home early enough for me to be in the Sunday morning service! I can't say the event was a miracle. It's possible (although rare) to have snowstorms in the middle of April in northern New Jersey. However, the storm came in direct response to my prayer! God chose to answer my prayer by His providence. Remember, miracles may be rare, but God's providences are not. As a person in crisis, does it really matter how God answers your prayer? For example, if I were diagnosed with a cancerous tumor, I wouldn't care whether God miraculously caused it to disappear by a miracle, or by His providence, enabled my white blood cells to gradually eat it up. The means wouldn't matter at all to me as long as the answer came. Take heart my friend, although miracles are rare, God's providences are not. Perhaps today is your day to experience a special providence of God.

Thoughts for today's meditation:

- Although miracles are rare, God's providences are not.
- God is capable of using the laws of nature to bring about His will in the circumstances of the believer.
- God has the power to alter your troubling circumstances.

Personal Reflections

Chapter 5
The Floodgates of Heaven

"So I say to you: Ask and it will be given to you; seek and you will find; knock and the door will be opened to you. For everyone who asks receives; he who seeks finds; and to him who knocks, the door will be opened." Luke 11:9-10.

Impossible situations can be overcome by prayer. In an impossible situation you often feel as if you need a door to open for you. You may be trapped by your circumstances and possibilities of escape just don't seem to exist. However, Jesus states in Luke 11:9-10, *"So I say to you: Ask and it will be given to you; seek and you will find; knock and the **door** will be opened to you"* (Emphasis added). Jesus Christ Himself assured us in this verse that God is in the business of opening doors for those who call on Him in prayer.

The Bible teaches that God not only opens doors but He is able to open "the floodgates of Heaven" for His children. The book of II King's relates the story of the siege of Samaria by the king of Aram (II Kings 6:24). The city was surrounded by a superior force with no way of escape and no way to get supplies in to its starving inhabitants. The famine was so severe that a donkey's head sold for 32oz. of silver. To start with, there isn't much meat on a donkey's head, but in addition, it was an unclean animal according to Jewish dietary law and they were forbidden to eat it. The famine was so severe that the Jews would break their dietary law and pay exorbitant prices for almost worthless meat. It would only be a matter of time before such degradation would be reached that the city would have to surrender. The men would likely be put to the sword and the women and children enslaved. The situation was indeed desperate.

The Bible recounts the story of a woman in the city who petitioned the king for justice (II King's 6:26-30). She had an agreement with a friend whereby they would actually eat each other's young sons. The famine had reached such a proportion that in their delirium, people actually considered eating their own children! In this particular case, the woman shared her son with her friend the previous day. When it came time for her friend to keep her end of the bargain and sacrifice her own child, she refused. The woman then went to the King for justice. He could do nothing but tear his robes in anguish of soul and walk away. Such was the degree of desperation in Samaria. All was hopeless.

At this juncture, the king of Samaria told the prophet Elisha, *"This disaster is from the Lord. Why should I wait for the Lord any longer?"* (II Kings 6:33b). Elisha replied that within 24 hours a seah of flour (7quarts) would sell for 2/5oz of silver and two seahs of barley would sell for the same amount (II Kings 7:1b). In response, one of the king's officers stated, *"Look, even if the Lord should open the floodgates of the heavens, could this happen?"* (II Kings 7:2b). The answer is of course it could. Nothing is impossible for God (Luke

1:37). At dusk, the Lord caused the Aramean army to hear the sound of chariots, horses and a great army rushing toward them (II Kings 7:6). They believed that the people of the city had somehow gotten word out to the Egyptians and Hittites and hired them to come to the rescue. In their panic, they fled camp for home leaving all of their supplies behind for the starving inhabitants of the city. All seemed lost but God did indeed open *"the floodgates of Heaven"* for His people!

The king of Samaria issued the challenge to Elisha, *"This disaster is from the Lord. Why should I wait for the Lord any longer?"* Likewise, you may be asking at this time, "Why should I wait for God any longer?" The answer, my friend, is you should wait on God because he is **able** to do the impossible. Remember, our perspective is limited as human beings but God's is not. No doubt the people of Samaria only saw two options from their limited perspective and neither was favorable. Option number one: face the superior force of the Aramean army in open confrontation and be slaughtered. Option number two: sue for peace and be either enslaved or slaughtered. There is no way they could have anticipated the marvelous way God would work in their favor. Therefore, we must not put God in a box. There are no limits to the possibilities of his workings. We must learn to trust Him and wait expectantly for Him to answer.   The psalmist said, *"…in the morning I lay my requests before you and wait in expectation"* (Psalm 5:3b). Similarly, we must **expect** answers from God.   Remember, God is in the business of opening doors in the midst of impossible circumstances. He opened the Red Sea for the Israelites and he opened the floodgates of Heaven for the Samaritans. What is the "Red Sea" you are up against right now? Put it before the Lord in prayer and give Him the chance to open "the floodgates of Heaven" for you!

Thoughts for today's meditation:

- God is in the business of opening doors for those who call on Him in prayer.
- Our perspective is limited as humans but God's is not. There are no limits to the possibilities of His workings.
- We must expect answers from God.

Personal Reflections

Chapter 6
Hurry Up and Wait!

"I am still confident of this: I will see the goodness of the Lord in the land of the living. Wait for the Lord; be strong and take heart and wait for the Lord." Psalm 27:13-14.

King David was a man who mastered the discipline of waiting on God and God blessed him beyond measure. He was anointed king of Israel by the prophet Samuel while he was still a teenage boy (I Samuel 16). Many years would pass before he entered his promised kingdom. In the interim, David served King Saul faithfully. However, Saul always saw him as a threat to his throne. He also knew that as long as David lived, his heir, Prince Jonathon would never become king. Therefore, Saul was jealous and took every opportunity to try to take David's life. Despite Saul's hatred for David and his attempts on his life, David refused to take matters into his own hands. Rather, he went into hiding and fled the wrath of Saul. God made him a promise and he relied on God alone to fulfill it. He would not raise his hand to shed the blood of the Lord's anointed king. On two occasions God seemed to deliver King Saul into the hands of David (I Samuel 24; 26). Each time his men urged him to kill him but he refused because Saul was God's anointed king over Israel. In each case, he spared Saul's life. A lesser man than David would have killed Saul and would not have lost any sleep over it. Killing Saul could be deemed self defense. However, David, "the man after God's own heart" (I Samuel 13:14), knew the value of waiting on God's timing. Had he taken vengeance, he would have lost the moral authority necessary for a unified kingdom. In God's time, Saul died in battle against Israel's enemies (I Samuel 31) and David became king over all of Judah (II Samuel 2) and later all of Israel (II Samuel 5).

During David's early years he had opportunities to usurp Saul's kingdom but he did not yield to the temptation. After slaying the Philistine giant, Goliath, the women of Israel came out of their towns as the army returned home dancing and singing, "Saul has slain his thousands, and David his tens of thousands." David could have capitalized on his popularity and sought to undermine Saul. In addition, David had the before mentioned opportunities to kill Saul. He could have allowed his mind to rationalize circumstances in order to justify usurping or killing Saul but he did not. He knew God to be faithful to his promises. He fully trusted God and waited for Him to fulfill His promise to him.

There is an understandable temptation during times of trial to be impatient; however, as we saw in the life of David, God blesses those who wait for His timing to bring about the answer to their prayers. It is an act of worship to wait on God. Waiting on God recognizes the fact that only He can meet your needs. In fact waiting is always associated with trials and trials are permitted by God to work the virtue of perseverance into the believer. James 1:2-4 states,

"Consider it pure joy, my brothers, whenever you face trials of many kinds, because you know that the testing of your faith develops perseverance. Perseverance must finish its work so that you may be mature and complete, not lacking anything." By the time David entered his kingdom, he was certainly "mature and complete, not lacking anything."

During times of trial, it helps to remember that God has a plan for your life as He did for David's and that plan is a plan to prosper you. God told the prophet Jeremiah, *"Before I formed you in the womb I knew you, before you were born, I set you apart..."* (Jeremiah 1:5). Later He stated, *"For I know the plans I have for you," declares the Lord, "plans to prosper you and not to harm you, plans to give you hope and a future"* (Jeremiah 29:11). These verses demonstrate to me that God knows us and loves us even before conception and that He already has a plan for our lives. Part of that plan involves trials to strengthen us. As a result of the years David spent in hiding and fleeing certain death at the hands of Saul, he developed a deep, abiding, trust and dependency on God which would enable him to be a good and wise king. The trials David went through prepared him for the fulfillment of God's promise to him. Early in his life, David may have been personally "ready" to be king; however, God had not yet "prepared" him to be king. There is a difference between being ready and being prepared. As you face your trial, think of it as a time of "preparation" for the great enlargement God has for your future. When the trial is over, you will be fully prepared to experience the blessing God has in store for you!

During a trial it is also important to remember that God is concerned about your desires. God created your innermost being (Psalm 139:13). I have to believe that this includes your thoughts, dreams, talents and desires. David stated in Psalm 37: 4, *"Delight yourself in the Lord and he will give you the desires of your heart."* He later stated, *"He fulfills the desires of those who fear him; he hears their cry and saves them"* (Psalm 145:19). The message is loud and clear; God is concerned with the desires of His children. Do you "delight" in the Lord? Do you "fear" (reverence) Him? If you do, you have a promise of God that He will grant your desires and you ought to pray expecting that he will! In Psalm 5:3 David wrote, *"In the morning, O Lord, you hear my voice; in the morning I lay my requests before you and wait in expectation"* (Emphasis added). It ought to be a great encouragement that David fully **expected** answers to his prayers. David never doubted that God would answer his prayers. In Psalm 27:13-14 he wrote, *"I am still confident of this: I will see the goodness of the Lord in the land of the living. Wait for the Lord; be strong and take heart and wait for the Lord"* (Emphasis added). David was absolutely confident that he would see the answers to his prayers in this life. He made his requests to God in the morning and waited expectantly for God to answer throughout the day. Some well meaning Christians say that David meant Heaven when he referred to the "land of the living" but that is not the case. He used the same phrase in Psalm 116:9 when he spoke of God rescuing him from death so that he could walk before Him *"in the land of the living."* Of course heaven is the ultimate answer to all of life's troubles, but David's life and writings teach us that we can expect God's deliverance in trials in **this** life!

Again, there is a temptation in any given trial to fail to wait on God's timing. This is illustrated in the account of David and Abigail in I Samuel 25. David and his men kept watch over the sheep and shepherds of a wealthy but surly landowner named Nabal while they were in hiding from Saul's army. David had 600 fighting men with him and this force acted as a wall protecting Nabal's property from thieves. When David sent messengers to asked Nabal for some food to sustain his men, Nabal refused and insulted him. David became enraged against him and swore, *"May God deal with David be it ever so severely if by morning I leave alive one male of all who belong to him!"* (I Samuel 25:22). At this point, Nabal's wife heard of David's plans and rushed toward his camp with food for his men hoping to appease his anger. Although her husband was a wicked man, and her life would no doubt be more pleasant without him, she brought food to David and petitioned him as she fell at his feet, *"My Lord, let the blame be on me alone ... Please forgive your servant's offense, for the Lord will certainly make a lasting dynasty for my master, because he fights the Lord's battles. Let no wrongdoing be found in you as long as you live"* (I Samuel 25:24, 28). David was conscience stricken and he praised Abigail's wisdom, *"May you be blessed for your good judgment and for keeping me from bloodshed this day and from avenging myself with my own hands"* (I Samuel 25:33). David put away his wrath and accepted the food Abigail and her servants brought and he turned away. Within ten days, Nabal was struck by the Lord and he died. Because David waited on God, he received the food his men needed and God avenged him of his enemy. He was now able to enter his promised kingdom without his conscience being tormented by bloodguilt. Because Abigail waited on God and didn't seek her wicked husband's demise, God gave her a new life with David who fell in love with her for her wisdom and beauty (I Samuel 25:3, 33, 39). Both waited on God and both received the desires of their hearts. Impatience only leads to sin and its consequences but patience and waiting on God brings joy and peace. The oft quoted Oswald Chambers once wrote, "Wait for God's time to bring it around and He will do it without any heartbreak or disappointment. When it is a question of the providential will of God, wait for God to move."[2] Amen!

Thoughts for today's meditation:

- God blesses those who wait for His timing to bring about the answer to their prayers.
- It is an act of worship to wait on God. Waiting on God recognizes the fact that only He can meet your needs.
- Waiting is always associated with trials and trials are permitted by God to work the virtues of patience and perseverance into the believer.
- During a trial it is also important to remember that God is concerned with your desires.

Personal Reflections

Chapter 7
Ask

"...You do not have, because you do not ask God." James 4:2d

As a father, I get a great deal of joy out of giving gifts to my children. That joy is heightened when I know that the gift I'm giving is something they desired, longed for and waited for for a long time. Nothing beats the excitement in those bright little eyes when the package is opened. "Oh Daddy, it's just what I've always wanted!" Oh, how it thrills my heart to hear those words and to know I've made one of my little ones happy. I have to believe that God feels the same way about His children. In fact, I'm certain that He does (Luke 11:9-13). God is our Heavenly Father and He delights in giving good gifts to His children. Sadly, many of God's children miss out on good gifts because they do not ask Him for things (James 4:2d). They feel that asking Him for things, especially for themselves, is selfish. This is not necessarily the case. God fully expects His children to ask Him for things. In fact, I submit, asking God for things is actually an act of worship. When you come to God with a request, you are acknowledging that only He can meet your need. You are confessing your reliance on Him and this is pleasing in His sight. You are precious to God. Why not ask him to meet that special need of your heart as His child?

When you ask God to grant the desire of your heart, do it with "childlike" faith. Children readily accept Daddy's word. They are believers, not skeptics. They are so innocent and so trusting. If Daddy says he's going to do something, then he is going to do it simply because he said he would. That is the kind of simple, innocent faith God expects of His children. In Mark 10:15 Jesus told His disciples, *"I tell you the truth, anyone who will not receive the kingdom of God like a little child will never enter it."* I am so glad Jesus doesn't require anything more than childlike faith to enter His Kingdom and I am so glad that He doesn't require anything more than childlike faith to have our prayers answered. Stop rationalizing God's promises and simply take them at face value in order to receive His blessings! Jesus also told His disciples, *"Therefore I tell you, whatever you ask for in prayer, believe that you have received it, and it will be yours"* (Mark 11:24). You need to believe you have already received what you have asked for. By the way, it's not necessarily the amount of your faith that matters; it is the object of your faith that matters. After all, it only takes faith in the amount of a mustard seed to move mountains according to Mathew 17:20. It is the object of your faith, God, who can do the impossible! (Luke 1:37).

In addition to praying in faith, God expects us to be persistent in prayer. Remember, you are his child and He delights in giving good gifts to His children. As a father, I know something of the persistence of children. At times it seems that all that matters in the entire world is a child's desire at the moment. This is most evident in my house at bedtime. My wife and I have four children and a dog. Getting things settled down at bedtime requires a great deal of skill. The girls get tucked in their room then Daddy prays with them and tucks the boys in and prays with them. And then I tiptoe to my room and slip under the covers anxiously anticipating sleep after a long day. It's at this point that "childlike" persistence begins. It begins as a long slow moan from the girl's room, "milllllllllllllllllllllllllllk." I initially ignore the moan thinking that perhaps it will fade as six year old Rebekah falls asleep.   However, it persists and increases in its volume and intensity, **"MILK! MILK! Milk! Milk! Milk!"** Finally, after much tossing and turning, I can no longer ignore the moans if I am to get any sleep so I get out of bed and get the milk.   Through "childlike" persistence, Rebekah, my precious little "Butterfly" gets her answer. I know it sounds simple, but it is a biblical concept. Jesus taught this principle in Luke 11:5-8.

Remember, Daddies have their little "Butterflies." As a child of God, you are God's precious "Butterfly". Why not worship your Daddy by coming to Him in prayer with the burning desire of your heart. Come to Him in "childlike" faith and with "childlike" persistence. He is a good Father and He delights in giving His children good gifts. Don't rationalize His promises; take them at face value and trust Him. If what you are praying for from a sincere heart is not in His will for you, in time, He will help you to see things from His perspective and change your mind about that thing you are praying for. However, until He does, expect an answer and be persistent! (see appendix 4 for my prayer for those who hurt).

Thoughts for today's meditation:

- God is a Good Father and delights in giving good gifts to His children.
- Asking God for things is actually a form of worship; it demonstrates your dependence on Him.
- God responds to "childlike" faith and "childlike" persistence.

Personal Reflections

Chapter 8
What if My "Trial" is My Fault?

"If the Lord delights in a man's way, he makes his steps firm; though he stumble, he will not fall, for the Lord upholds him with his hand."
Psalm 37:23-24

Sadly, more often than not, the trials we face in our lives are the result of sin or poor decisions on our part. Rest assured, even in these situations the Lord cares and will not forsake you. The nation Israel, the apple of God's eye in the Bible, turned away from Him many times and His response was, *"Can a mother forget the baby at her breast and have no compassion on the child she has born? Though she may forget, I will not forget you!"* (Isaiah 49:15). What a beautiful statement! There is no stronger bond in this world than that between a mother and her child. God promises you that His love for you is even stronger. It doesn't matter what kind of trouble you find yourself in, God will never forsake you. He is there for you and He will carry you through.

The prophet Jonah experienced a crisis because he ran away from God. God wanted him to go to the Assyrian city of Nineveh to preach against it (Jonah 1:1-2). Jonah, however, had other plans. He disobeyed God and went to the port city of Joppa on Israel's Mediterranean coast. At Joppa, Jonah paid for passage on a ship bound for Tarshish. Tarshish was at the opposite end of the Mediterranean Sea on the coast of Spain. In effect, Jonah was waving his finger in the face of God. Tarshish was at the end of the known world at the time and was about as far away from Nineveh as one could get. Jonah was probably angry at God because the Ninevites had destroyed Jerusalem and he had no desire to preach to them and see them come to repentance. He was a very bitter man.

Soon after Jonah's ship set sail, the Lord sent a violent storm which threatened to break it apart (Jonah 1:4). During the storm, the sailors each cried out to their gods pleading for help. They threw the cargo overboard to lighten the ship's load and then they began to cast lots in order to determine who was responsible for the calamity they were in and the lot fell on Jonah. When the lot fell on Jonah the crew asked, *"Tell us, who is responsible for making all this trouble for us...?"* (Jonah 1:8). Jonah explained that he was running away from *"the God of heaven, who made the sea and the land"* (Jonah 1:9). This terrified the crew and they asked him what they should do to him to calm the sea. Jonah responded, *"Pick me up and throw me into the sea ... and it will become calm. I know that it is my fault that this great storm has come upon you"* (Jonah 1:12 emphasis added). Jonah knew, without a doubt, that the calamity the ship faced was due to **his** actions. He ran away from God and there were consequences. His sin created a storm that affected others around him. Perhaps an indiscretion has created a storm in your life as it did Jonah's. Perhaps the storm in your life is affecting others around you. Jonah's story may be your story my friend. Take heart, God did not forsake him and He will not forsake you either!

Although Jonah despaired and told the men of the ship to throw him overboard, God provided a great fish to swallow him. Whatever kind of fish (sea creature) it was, it was large enough to swallow a man whole along with enough air to keep him alive for three days because Jonah spent three days and nights in its belly (Jonah 1:17). In Jonah's distress, he called out to the Lord (prayed) and God commanded the fish to spit him up onto dry land (Jonah 2:2,10). On land, God spoke to Jonah a second time directing him to go to Nineveh to preach against it. This time he obeyed (Jonah 3:1-3). In the end, God used Jonah's preaching to bring a city of 120,000 people to repentance and faith in God. Even though he disobeyed God and ran from Him, God did not forsake him. God could have killed Jonah and raised up another prophet to preach to Nineveh, but He did not. Like a mother, who cannot forget the nursing babe at her breast, God did not forget Jonah. God graciously brought circumstances into his life which brought him back in line with His will. Jonah learned more in the belly of the great fish than any seminary could ever teach him.   He learned and experienced the grace of God. Are you running from God? Are you ignoring His still small voice? Why not yield yourself to His will and find the peace and purpose that Jonah found without experiencing his suffering? Perhaps you are in the belly of the fish right now, why not cry out to God as Jonah did? God will hear and He will respond. He loves you!

King David was another man of God who found himself facing crisis because of his own sin. The books of II Samuel Chapters 11 and 12 recount the history of his notorious sin with the beautiful Bathsheba. While the armies of Israel were off at war, David stayed behind. One evening, he got up out of bed and took a stroll along the top of the wall of his palace when his eyes fell upon the angelic form of Bathsheba bathing. Consumed with passion, he sent for her and committed adultery with her (Bathsheba was married). In time, David received word that she was pregnant and in an effort to hide his sin, he called her husband, Uriah, back from the battle lines. Adding to the depravity of the sin, Uriah was a trusted friend of David and one of his legendary "30 mighty men" (II Samuel 23:39). When Uriah arrived at the palace, David did everything he could to get him to go home and spend the night with his wife. He had hoped that he would sleep with her and that the pregnancy would appear to be his. Uriah, however, refused to go home and enjoy its comforts while his men were in the field fighting the Lord's battles. This enraged David who then sent Uriah back to the front carrying a sealed letter to General Joab, *"Put Uriah in the front line where the fighting is fiercest. Then withdraw from him so he will be struck down and die"* (II Samuel 11:15). Joab did just that and Uriah was killed. After Bathsheba finished mourning for her husband, David sent for her and they were married. David may have thought he was successful in hiding his sin, but nothing escapes the eyes of God and God was not pleased. He sent the prophet Nathan to confront David (II Samuel 12:1-14). When Nathan arrived, he related the story of a rich man in David's kingdom with an abundance of flocks who had taken a lamb from a poor man to feed a guest. The poor man's lamb was all he had and it was treated as a family pet even eating at his table. On hearing this, David was enraged and said, *"As surely as the Lord lives, the man who did this deserves to die! He must pay for that lamb four times over, because he did such a thing and had no pity"* (II Samuel 12:5-6). Nathan responded in the following verse by stating emphatically, *"You are the man!"* David must have been mortified at this moment. His sin was exposed. Nathan then said, *"...This is what the Lord, the God of Israel, says: 'I anointed you king over Israel, and I delivered you from the hand of Saul. I gave your master's house to you, and your master's wives into your arms. I gave you the house of Israel and Judah. And if all of this had been too little, I would have given you even more. Why did you despise the word of the Lord by doing what is evil in his eyes?"* (II Samuel 12:7-9 emphasis added). God expressed His displeasure with David and reminded him that if all he had given him was too little, all he had to do as a child of God was ask for more. He did not have to "despise" the word of the Lord by breaking His commandments to get what he wanted.

In shame, David repented and the Lord took away his sin (II Samuel 12:13), however, he was punished ironically, four times over for his sins of adultery and murder. His punishment (II Samuel 12:10-14) included:

1. The sword (war) never left his household.

2. His son Absalom rebelled against him in an effort to kill him and take his kingdom.
3. Absalom took and slept with his wives publicly
4. The child conceived by Bathsheba died.

Despite, the terrible punishment God carried out against David, He was exceedingly merciful. David's life was spared and his rule over the kingdom preserved. God was even merciful to Bathsheba. Although her first child died, her second by David, Solomon, became David's heir and Israel's wisest and richest king. He would also be in the genealogy of the Messiah, Jesus Christ (Mathew 1:6). David's sins were among the worst a man could commit, adultery and murder. Both of these sins were against a trusted friend, Uriah. However, God is the greatest recycler the world has ever known! When we repent, as David did, He is able to take the junk of our lives and recycle it into something wonderful! David's sin produced Psalm 51 (see appendix 3). This Psalm is his psalm of confession which has provided both comfort and a model for true repentance for millions through the ages. It also produced Solomon, Israel's prolific writer of wisdom literature including the books of Proverbs, Ecclesiastes and Song of Solomon. I am always overcome with emotion when I think that this wise and accomplished king was raised and taught at the feet of a woman who would otherwise be despised by the world for her sin. God is so gracious! It doesn't matter what depth of depravity you may have sunk to my friend, if you repent, God can and will **raise you up!** He will not only raise you up but He will recycle the junk of your life into something wonderful and make you a blessing to others!

Thoughts for today's meditation:

- Even when we fall God does not forsake us.
- We should never "despise" the word of the Lord in order to get what we want. We should ask Him to meet the desires of our hearts.
- God is the greatest recycler the world has ever known. When we repent, He is able to take the "junk" of our lives and turn it into something wonderful!

Personal Reflections

Personal Reflections

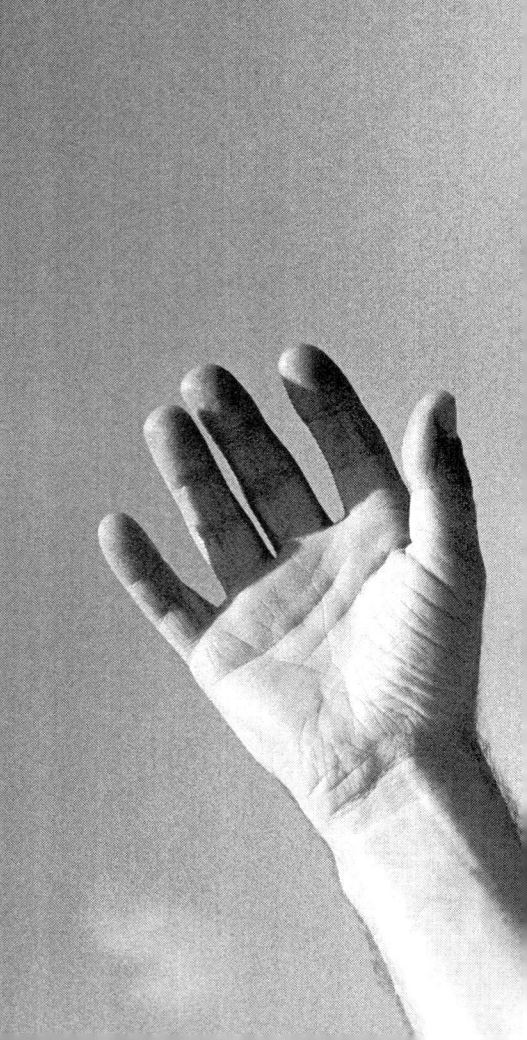

Chapter 9
Hearing the Voice of God

"My sheep listen to my voice; I know them, and they follow me" John 10:27

In John 10:27 Jesus said, *"My sheep listen to my voice; I know them, and they follow me."* Jesus was using an illustration that would have been readily understood by the people in Jerusalem He was speaking to. They were very familiar with shepherding. They would often see flocks of sheep grazing in the fields outside of the city. They were acquainted with the way shepherds grazed their flocks in common fields. As the sheep grazed, they mingled with and became indistinguishable from the sheep of other shepherds. As each individual shepherd left for the day, he gave his own unique call to his sheep which melted out of the crowd in response to his voice. Jesus told the people of Jerusalem that it is the same with His sheep. They hear His voice and they know Him. It is therefore a biblical truth that God speaks to His children and that His sheep hear his voice.

How is it that God speaks to His children? He does it by His Holy Spirit which indwells each believer (John 14:15-17). The Spirit of God often "checks" the believer's soul in much the same way a master might "check" his dog by jerking his leash when he is going the wrong way. When a believer feels this "check" in his spirit, he needs to reconsider the direction he is taking. Alternatively, the Holy Spirit can also prompt the spirit of the believer to action. For example, the believer might be conscience stricken to act with compassion towards someone or even to make a particular decision or take a particular action.

God also speaks through His written word as it is read or preached. This is the safest way to hear the voice of God because little is left up to interpretation. However, it has been my personal experience that the voice of God often goes beyond the original audience of the actual passage and is "re-spoken" by the Holy Spirit to the reader in a particular set of circumstances. For example, in 2007 I was embroiled in a church/state controversy which became a media circus. It was the first full week of school in my junior level, accelerated US History class and the discussions centered on current events. During the course of the discussions, an atheist student began asking controversial questions and recorded my responses without my knowledge. He then went to the administration and shortly afterwards, to 300 media outlets with the recordings. I had done nothing wrong; I just gave honest answers to what I believed were sincere questions about what the Bible says about God. In short, my job of 15 years was in jeopardy. I had received a letter from the superintendant of schools which explained that my employment would be discussed at the next board of education meeting. The night before the meeting, as you might have already guessed, I was uneasy. I was concerned I might lose my job, and along with it, my health insurance. This was especially troubling because my youngest child, Hannah (age 2), was diagnosed with a serious kidney disease. In the middle of the night I woke up out of a restless sleep and picked up my Bible looking for comfort. I let it fall open and the first verse my eyes were drawn to was Psalm 12:5b, *"I will now arise, says the Lord. I will protect them from those who malign them."* These words seemed to be spoken directly to me from God Himself. I was overcome with peace and was able to sleep like a baby. The next day, 150 people rose to my defense during the school board meeting where I was being persecuted for my faith. God silenced my accusers just like He told me He would through His written word "re-spoken" to my heart.

On another occasion, I had to make an important decision. I was completely paralyzed with indecision. I knew what I wanted but wasn't sure what God wanted. In any case, whatever decision I made, people would be hurt. I decided to pray and trust God's promise in James 1:5, *"If any of you lacks wisdom, he should ask God, who gives generously to all without finding fault, and it will be given to him."* Within a day of my prayer, as I opened a Bible seeking comfort from God, Psalm 4:5 (as written in the NAS version) seemed to leap off the page. The verse reads, *"Offer the sacrifices of righteousness and trust the Lord."* God's message to me was loud and clear. I needed to offer God a sacrifice of righteousness. In this particular instance, I had to do what was "right" not what I desired if peace was ever to be brought to my situation. I had to learn to trust God with everything, including the most earnest desires of my heart.

I have also found that God often speaks through circumstances. Job is an example of a man who experienced this. As a man, God said of him, *"There is no one on earth like him; he is blameless and upright, a man who fears God and shuns evil"* (Job 1:8b). Humanly speaking, you would think that a man like Job should be exempt from trials. However, "...the Lord disciplines those he loves..." (Proverbs 3:12a). Remember, discipline is **teaching**, not punishment. Job was not being punished, but being trained, tested and stretched to the end that he would come to a fuller understanding of God and have a more intimate fellowship with Him. Calamity overtook Job like a cyclone (Job 1). He lost his wealth, his servants, all seven of his children and eventually his health (Job 2). Through it all he refused to curse God (Job 2:9-10). He questioned God but never cursed or blamed Him. In the end, after Job's lengthy season of painful trial, he was able to say, *"My ears had heard of you but now my eyes have seen you..."* (Job 42:5). Job, no doubt, learned about the living God through the teachings of his parents and the elders among his people. He had indeed **heard** of God. It was the intense fires trial however which enabled Job to **see** God. Job saw God in His circumstances and God spoke to Him through His circumstances. What might God be saying to you through your circumstances? Listen well and take heart. At the end of Job's trial God blessed him with **twice** as much as He had given him before and blessed the latter part of his life more than the first (Job 42:10, 12a). Maintain hope and persevere, He can certainly do the same for you.

In addition to circumstances, I have found that God speaks to us through signs given in answer to prayer. For example, when it was time for the patriarch Abraham to find a suitable wife for his son Isaac, he commissioned a servant with this important task. The servant, understanding the gravity of his mission was fearful of making the wrong choice. He therefore prayed for a sign which would make the choice clear and he worshipped God when he received the sign he asked for in his prayer (Genesis 24:12-18). The sign given in this passage confirmed that God would be faithful to the promise He made Abraham and the servant. I have had similar experiences in answer to prayer. I have prayed for specific signs in accordance with Psalm 86:17, *"Give me a sign of your goodness..."* In some cases God fulfilled them in unmistakable detail. I took the answers as the voice of God confirming that my request would be met. There have been some that haven't been fulfilled yet, but because He gave the specific sign I requested, I continue to wait in expectation for the fulfillment of God's promises to me.

In your trial my friend, remember, God is present. He indwells you by His Spirit. Listen and you will hear His voice giving you the answer, direction or comfort you need!

Thoughts for today's meditation:

- God speaks by His Holy Spirit which indwells the believer.
- God speaks through His written Word as it is read or preached.

- The voice of God often goes beyond the original audience of the text of the Bible and is "re-spoken" to the believer by the Holy Spirit in a particular set of circumstances.
- God sometimes speaks to us through circumstances and signs given in answer to prayer.

Personal Reflections

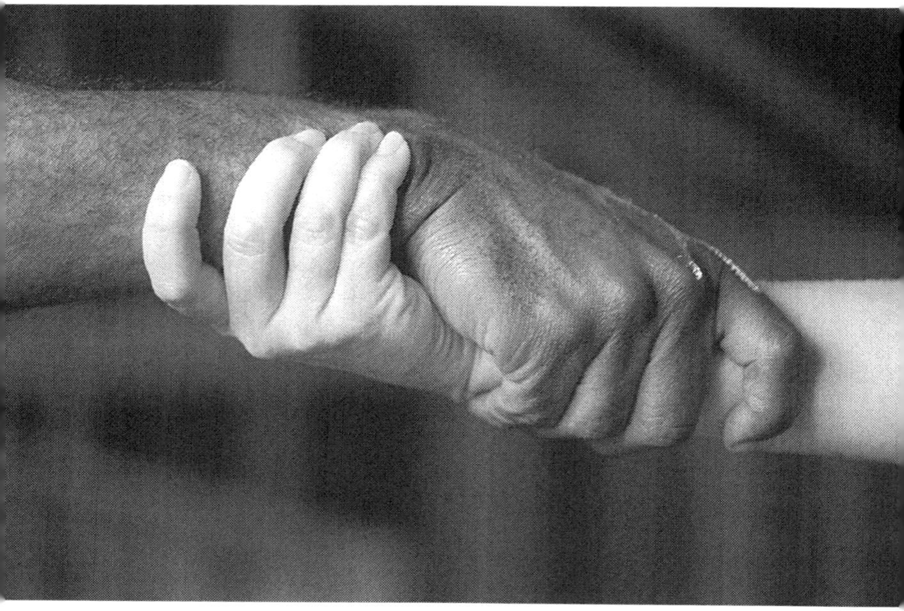

Chapter 10
Trusting the Promises of God

"The Lord is Faithful to all his promises..." Psalm 145:13b

One of the most comforting attributes of God for the individual who is in crisis is the fact that He is bound by His promises. Not only is He bound by His promises but circumstances cannot prevent Him from keeping them. As a father, there have been times I made promises to my children. Sadly, despite my best intentions, there were times circumstances prevented me from keeping them. **Nothing** hurts more than not being able to keep a promise due to circumstances. It hurts because you know you let down someone you love. This is never an issue for God, however, because He is in control of circumstances and He can alter them by a mere act of His will. Even those things that appear to be chance happenings are really part of His sovereign will (Proverbs 16:33). God either caused the circumstances to occur or He allowed them to take place for one reason or another.

God is not just in control of our circumstances, He is completely trustworthy. The Bible says, *"God is not a man, that he should lie, nor a son of man, that He should change His mind. Does he speak and then not act? Does he promise and not fulfill?"* (Numbers 23:19). God is completely trustworthy! He does not lie and He doesn't change His mind. We can therefore fully trust the promises He gives (see appendix 2 for a list of God's promises). As humans, it is natural for our faith in God to waver at times. There are times we need reassurance. There was an occasion when I asked God for something very specific in prayer. I prayed believing and felt my prayer was accepted by Him. After some time I began to doubt and I prayed for a sign which would confirm that God was going to indeed answer my prayer in the affirmative in the future. Within hours, God granted me the exact sign I asked for. I was elated! I felt I had heard the voice of God in answer to my prayer! However, as the weeks went on, doubts began to flood my mind again. I began to doubt whether God had spoken to me at all and that perhaps I wasn't going to receive what I believed He had promised. In my anguish of soul I begged God to reconfirm His promise to me. Graciously, He answered by impressing a verse of Scripture on my heart and mind, *"What I have said, that will I bring about; what I have planned, that will I do"* (Isaiah 46:11b). Once again I was elated! God reassured me that I not only heard his voice, but that He was going to bring about exactly what He said He would. This reassurance gave me peace and left me loving God even more! Some might feel that God does not work this way, however, we have the example of Gideon in Judges chapter six. Gideon was threshing wheat when God visited him and told him He would use him to deliver the Israelites from their overlords, the Midianites. Gideon doubted that God had actually spoken to him and asked for reassurance through a sign. God granted the sign and in time Gideon began to doubt again. He asked God for another sign for reassurance, *"...If you will save Israel by my hand as you have promised-- look, I will place a wool fleece on the threshing floor. If there is dew only on the fleece and all the ground is dry, then I will know that you will save Israel by my hand as you said"* (Judges 6:36). In the next verse we learn that that is exactly what happened. God reassured Gideon by granting him the exact sign he asked for. Later, in verse 39, in a moment of weakness, Gideon tested the Lord again, *"...Do not be angry with me. Let me make just one more request. Allow me one more test with the fleece. This time make the fleece dry and the ground covered with dew."* In the next verse we learn that that is exactly what God did! Although Gideon was weak and experienced doubt, God did not forsake him. He will not forsake you either. He is always, always, always faithful to His promises! In your crisis my friend, meditate on God's promises. He will not let you down. Perhaps He has spoken to your heart and made you a personal promise. Take Him at His word and remember, the fulfillment of the promise is guaranteed because of His faithfulness not because of yours.

Thoughts for today's meditation:

- God is bound by His promises and circumstances do not prevent Him from keeping them.
- God is in control of our circumstances and He can alter them by a mere act of His will.
- The fulfillment of God's promises is guaranteed because of His faithfulness not yours.

Personal Reflections

Personal Reflections

Chapter 11
Faith is "Cutting the Ropes"

"Now faith is being sure of what we hope for and certain of what we do not see." Hebrews 11:1

Faith is arguably the single most important doctrine in Christianity, yet it is probably the most misunderstood. According to the Bible, *"...faith is being **sure** of what we hope for and **certain** of what we do not see"* (Hebrews 11:1 emphasis added). Faith is being **confident** that God is **able** to keep His promises and that He **will**, in fact, keep His promises. It is of vital importance to the believer because without it is impossible to please God (Hebrews 11:6). The benefits of faith are: salvation from sin (Ephesians 2:8-9), justification before God (Genesis 15:6) and answered prayer (Mark 11:24). The wonderful thing about faith is that it is available to all and it doesn't take much to move the hand of God. Jesus Himself said, *"...I tell you the truth, if you have faith as small as a mustard seed, you can say to this mountain, 'Move from here to there' and it will move. Nothing will be impossible for you"* (Mathew 17:20). It doesn't take much faith to move mountains. Jesus doesn't require you to have the faith of Billy Graham or Mother Teresa. He requires you to have faith the size of a very small seed and like a seed, your faith will grow and grow as it is tried and tested. What are the mountains (obstacles) you face? By faith, they can be moved out of the way!

If you want your faith to grow, you have to read the Bible. The Apostle Paul said, *"For everything that was written in the past was written to teach us, so that through endurance and encouragement of the Scriptures we might have hope"* (Romans 15:4). Everything written in the Scriptures, therefore, was written to teach us, encourage us and give us hope! If you are going through a crisis, you certainly need encouragement and hope and the Bible is the source. As you read how God worked in the lives of His children responding to their needs and answering their prayers, you gain hope. Faith is also increased by hearing the Word of God, *"Consequently, faith comes from hearing the message, and the message is heard through the word of Christ"* (Romans 10:17). In addition to Bible reading, a believer's faith is also strengthened by hearing God's Word preached.

Acts chapter 27 has an excellent account of how faith works. The Apostle Paul was arrested for preaching the Gospel. He was under guard on a ship to Italy where he was to make an appeal to Caesar. Before the ship left the island of Crete for Italy Paul warned the crew, *"Men, I can see that our voyage is going to be disastrous and bring great loss to the ship and cargo, and to our own lives also"* (Acts 27:10). The crew failed to heed Paul's prophetic warning and ended up lost at sea in a violent "northeaster" with hurricane force winds. They were in total darkness for days. Without the aid of the sun, moon and stars they could not get a bearing and did not know where they were. The sails were taken down and ropes were passed under the hull of the ship to keep it from breaking apart under the force of the waves. The anchor was let out in hopes of catching hold if in the darkness the ship was blown into shallow water. All cargo and tackle were thrown overboard in order to lighten the ship and keep it afloat. There was little food left and on the 14th day they were still in total darkness. It seemed all was lost. When depth readings were taken, they were in 90 feet of water and feared being crushed upon rocks. At this point, an angel visited Paul and said, *"Do not be afraid Paul. You must stand trial before Caesar; and God has graciously given you the lives of all who sail with you"* (Acts 27:24). Paul shared the news with the crew in an effort to encourage them. He stated, *"...I have faith in God that it will happen just as he told me"* (Acts 27:25). However, in an attempt to secretly escape the ship, the sailors let the lifeboat down into the sea, pretending to lower some anchors. When Paul observed this attempt to escape the ship, he said to the centurion and soldiers guarding him, *"Unless these men stay with the ship, you cannot be saved"* (Acts 27:31). Hearing Paul's admonition, the soldiers took a very gutsy step of faith and cut the ropes to the lifeboat letting it fall away! The lifeboat was their only earthly hope of survival, yet they cut it loose! When the seasoned veterans of the sea, the sailors, thought all was lost and were ready to abandon ship, by faith, the soldiers cut the ropes! As a result, all 276 passengers on board were saved. **Faith is cutting the ropes!**

What is the lifeboat you are clinging to in your crisis right now? What do you trust in besides God? Are you trying to manipulate circumstances in order to have

your own way? Do you trust in your own strength?
Whatever that lifeboat is, cut it loose and trust God
alone. He will not let you down!

Thoughts for today's meditation:

- Faith is being confident that God is able to keep
  His promises and that He will, in fact, keep His
  promises.
- Without faith, it is impossible to please God.
- Faith grows by reading and hearing the word of
  God.
- Faith is "cutting the ropes."

Personal Reflections

Chapter 12
The Hope of the Resurrection

"...I am the resurrection and the life. He who believes in me will live, even though he dies."
John 11:25

When in crisis, you can trust Jesus Christ, the God of the Bible. He is absolutely trustworthy and the basis of this assurance is the fact of His resurrection from the dead. He never expected his followers to believe blindly. He told them that if they didn't believe His words, to at least believe the evidence of the miracles themselves (John. 14:11). Jesus authenticated His message and identity by performing miracles. The greatest of these miracles was His resurrection from the dead. There are two amazing aspects to this miracle. First, He predicted it in advance (Mathew 16:21; Mark 10:33-34; Luke 9:22). Second, it actually happened (Acts 2:23-24; 3:13-15). Taken by itself, the resurrection is already a singularity. However, given the fact that it was predicted in detail by Jesus Himself one week prior makes it the greatest miracle of the Bible. The very God of the universe, who created man, emptied Himself of his former glory and took on human flesh. He set aside the independent use of his attributes as God and allowed Himself to be fully human. As such, he died on a cross as the atonement for man's sins. In order to confirm who He was, He predicted His death and resurrection in detail one week in advance.

Jesus put a premium on evidence for His claims about himself. Both His prophecy concerning His resurrection as well as the resurrection itself confirm this.

God the Father is equally interested in providing man with evidence for his faith. Acts 17:31 makes it clear that one of God's purposes in raising Jesus from the dead was to provide "proof" of man's coming judgment. In addition, in regard to the evidentiary value of the resurrection, we must remember that God could have very easily just said He loved us. However, it seems, in some sense, emotions like this have to be played out in space and time for them to be real. For example, a father can say his children are his priority, but if he never spends time with them, his actions prove otherwise. God didn't just say He loved us, He proved it by entering space and time and dying for us. He "evidenced" his love for us. God doesn't expect His children to believe blindly, He provides them with evidence to support their faith in Him.

Consider the empty tomb of Jesus as evidence for the resurrection. There are essentially only four plausible explanations for the empty tomb offered by scholars:

1. **The disciples stole the body:**
   The disciples had nothing to gain by stealing the body. They certainly gained no worldly benefits from preaching the resurrection; tradition tells us they were martyred for testifying to the fact of the resurrection.

2. **The Jews stole the body:**
   The idea here is that the Jews stole it so that the disciples couldn't claim the resurrection. If this were the case, those same Jews could have very easily produced the body of Jesus in order to refute the disciples' claims when they preached He was risen.

3. **Jesus was in a coma like state in the tomb:**
   The Jesus who died by crucifixion would be in no shape to convince anyone that he had been raised from the dead. He would obviously be alive, but not raised in glory. He would have been ragged in appearance from the flogging he received.

4. **The women who first saw the empty tomb went to the wrong tomb:**
   The women (at least Mary Magdalene and Mary the mother of Joses) witnessed the entombment of Jesus (Mathew 27:61; Mark 15:47; Luke 23:55). It would be highly unlikely that they would go to the wrong tomb as a result. In addition, the Gospel of John states that the tomb was in a garden near Calvary (John 19:41:42). It is highly unreasonable that the women went to the wrong tomb. If in fact they forgot the way in the two days since the burial, it would have been very easily distinguished from the others. It was the one sealed and guarded by Roman troops (Mathew 27:65, 66).

There are those who claim that the resurrection of Jesus cannot be proven with certainty. I agree that the resurrection cannot be proven beyond doubt; however, I believe it can be proven beyond a "reasonable" doubt. Proof beyond a reasonable doubt is proof so convincing that you would act on it. You would act on it in your own affairs without reservation. Allow me to share an illustration I heard years ago given by a judge.[3] Suppose you woke up at 8:00am and went to the kitchen to look out your window. Upon looking out the window you notice four inches of snow on the ground. Because there was no snow on the ground the night before, you would reasonably assume that it snowed while you were sleeping. It would be unreasonable to suggest that that little green Martians with snow machines put the snow there while you were sleeping. Is it possible, I suppose, but it is unreasonable? Likewise, you leave the window for five minutes to brush your teeth. When you come back you notice cat paw prints in the snow. You could therefore reasonably assume that a cat walked by the window in the snow in the five minutes you were gone. It would be unreasonable to assume that those same space aliens walked by on cat stilts for the purpose of deceiving you. Is it possible? I suppose, but it is unreasonable.

With regard to Jesus of Nazareth, His resurrection can be accepted beyond any reasonable doubt. In the absence of a legitimately plausible explanation for the empty tomb, one must accept the fact that Jesus raised Himself from the dead proving Himself to be God and we can therefore trust **all** of His **promises** to us including the promise that we too will one day be resurrected (I Thessalonians 4:13-18).

Thoughts for today's meditation:

- Jesus' resurrection can be accepted beyond any reasonable doubt.
- Jesus Christ is absolutely trustworthy and the basis of that assurance is the fact of His resurrection from the dead.
- Jesus proved Himself to be God by His resurrection; therefore, we can trust **all** of His **promises** to us.

Personal Reflections

Notes

[i] A.W. Tozer, The Root of the Righteous (Harrisburg, PA: Christian Publications, 1955) 137.

[ii] Oswald Chambers, My Utmost For His Highest (Uhrichsville, Ohio: Barbour Publishing Inc) Jan. 4.

[iii] I heard this illustration given by Michael William Lebron, "Lionel", in the mid 1990s on WABC 770 AM. I thought it was outstanding. WABC is a news – talk station in NYC.

Bible Versions

Unless otherwise stated, all Scripture quotations are from The New International Version. Copyright 1973, 1978, 1984 by International Bible Society.

New American Standard Bible, Copyright 1960, 1962, 1963, 1971, 1972, 1973, 1975, 1977 by The Lockman Foundation.

Appendix 1
Steps to becoming a child of God:

1. **Understand that you are a sinner in need of a Savior**

   "for all have sinned and fall short of the glory of God." Romans 3:23

2. **Understand that the wages of sin is death.**

   "For the wages of sin is death..." Romans 6:23a

3. **Understand that God gave His Son as a sacrifice for sin in your place.**

   "...but the gift of God is eternal life in Christ Jesus our Lord." Romans 6:23b

   "But God demonstrates his own love for us in this: While we were still sinners, Christ died for us." Romans 5:8

4. **Understand that in order to be forgiven, you need to accept the finished work of Jesus and call out to Him for salvation.**

   "That if you confess with your mouth, "Jesus is Lord," and believe in your heart that God raised him from the dead, you will be saved." Romans 10:9

For, "Everyone who calls on the name of the Lord will be saved." Romans 10:13

If you would like to trust Christ as your Savior and become a child of God, why not pray the following prayer from a sincere heart:

Dear Jesus, I know that I am a sinner. I also know that you are God and that you died on the cross for my sins. I also know that you rose again on the third day. Please forgive me of my sins and make me one of your children. Thank you Jesus, amen.

Appendix 2
Some of God's Many Promises for Heavy Hearts

God Keeps His Promises

Psalm 145:13b
"The Lord is faithful to all his promises and loving to all he has made."

II Corinthians 1:20
"For no matter how many promises God has made, they are yes in Christ."

Numbers 23:19
"God is not a man, that he should lie, nor a son of man, that he should change his mind. Does he speak and then not act? Does he promise and not fulfill?"

Isaiah 46:11b
"What I have said, that will I bring about; what I have planned, that will I do."

God Cares about Your Desires

Psalm 37:4
"Delight yourself in the LORD and he will give you the desires of your heart."

Psalm 145:19
"He fulfills the desires of those who fear him; he hears

their cry and saves them."

God Cares about your Pain

Psalm 147:3
"He heals the brokenhearted and binds up their wounds. "

God Answers Prayer

Mark 11:24
"Therefore I tell you, whatever you ask for in prayer, believe that you have received it, and it will be yours."

God Forgives Your Sins

I John 1:9
"If we confess our sins, he is faithful and just and will forgive us our sins and purify us from all unrighteousness."

God Has a Wonderful Plan for Your Life

Jeremiah 29:11
"For I know the plans I have for you," declares the LORD, "plans to prosper you and not to harm you, plans to give you hope and a future."

Appendix 3
King David's model for confession and repentance:

Psalm 51

For the director of music. A psalm of David. When the prophet Nathan came to him after David had committed adultery with Bathsheba.

[1] Have mercy on me, O God, according to your unfailing love; according to your great compassion blot out my transgressions.

[2] Wash away all my iniquity and cleanse me from my sin.

[3] For I know my transgressions, and my sin is always before me.

[4] Against you, you only, have I sinned and done what is evil in your sight, so that you are proved right when you speak and justified when you judge.

[5] Surely I was sinful at birth, sinful from the time my mother conceived me.

[6] Surely you desire truth in the inner parts; you teach me wisdom in the inmost place.

[7] Cleanse me with hyssop, and I will be clean; wash me, and I will be whiter than snow.

[8] Let me hear joy and gladness; let the bones you have crushed rejoice.

[9] Hide your face from my sins and blot out all my iniquity.

[10] Create in me a pure heart, O God, and renew a

steadfast spirit within me.

[11] Do not cast me from your presence or take your Holy Spirit from me.

[12] Restore to me the joy of your salvation and grant me a willing spirit, to sustain me.

[13] Then I will teach transgressors your ways, and sinners will turn back to you.

[14] Save me from bloodguilt, O God, the God who saves me, and my tongue will sing of your righteousness.

[15] O Lord, open my lips, and my mouth will declare your praise.

[16] You do not delight in sacrifice, or I would bring it; you do not take pleasure in burnt offerings.

[17] The sacrifices of God are a broken spirit; a broken and contrite heart, O God, you will not despise.

[18] In your good pleasure make Zion prosper; build up the walls of Jerusalem.

[19] Then there will be righteous sacrifices, whole burnt offerings to delight you; then bulls will be offered on your altar.

Appendix 4
Notes on Psalm 20:1-4

The Psalms are prayers and praises to God which were sung. I have found it to be a rewarding exercise to meditate on them and pray them as I read them. Psalm 20:1-4 is my favorite. I pray it daily for myself as well as for others. In your crisis, why not meditate on these four verses and pray them for yourself?

1 May the LORD answer you when you are in distress; may the name of the God of Jacob protect you.

David could have chosen any number of names for God for this Psalm but he chose to use "God of Jacob." This gives me great comfort. Jacob was a very selfish, sinful man but God loved him and answered his prayers. Jacob was a manipulator (Gen. 25:26; 27-33). He was also a deceiver (Gen. 27:1-29). Despite Jacob's sinfulness, God blessed him. In fact, Jacob wrestled with God (Gen. 32:22-29) and prevailed! He would not let go of Him until He blessed him and God did! If God could bless Jacob, He can certainly bless me!

2 May he send you help from the sanctuary and grant you support from Zion.

Prayer:
Oh Lord, please hear me in my distress and set my feet securely on high. I am nothing more than a sinful deceiver. However, I take comfort in knowing that you

blessed your servant Jacob who was a deceiver like me. I know that Jacob wrestled with you and would not let you go without a blessing. Father, please help me not to let go as I wrestle you in prayer. I desperately need your blessing!

I am also reminded how God sent Daniel help immediately in answer to his prayer (Daniel 9:21-23). God "sent" the angel Gabriel in "swift flight" to endow Daniel with wisdom and later "strength" (Daniel10:18).

Prayer:
Oh Lord, please dispatch your angel in swift flight to touch me and give me strength and wisdom. I feel faint and need your strength oh Lord my God. Please have mercy on me as you did your servant Daniel.

3 May he remember all your sacrifices and accept your burnt offerings.

This verse reminds me of Hezekiah's plea for healing from God when he was terminally ill. He begged God to remember his faithfulness, service and devotion to Him as he asked Him for healing. God relented and answered his prayer (II King's20:1-6).

Prayer:
Precious Father, please remember all of my service and devotion to you from my youth. Please count my tears and weigh them on your balance. Please remember my

suffering and accept this offering of prayer

4 May he give you the desire of your heart and make all your plans succeed.

God is interested in my desires! Psalm 139 tells me that He "created my inmost being!" He knows my desires and he delights in meeting my desires (Psalm 37:4; 145:19).

Prayer:
Gracious, Heavenly Father, you know the desires of my heart. Please be merciful to me and grant me the desires of my heart as you did your servant David (Psalm 21:2). Your Word says that you are "...faithful to all of your promises..." (Ps. 145:13b). I believe you Father and I am trusting you. Please strengthen me and help me overcome my unbelief (Mark 9:24).

Amen and Amen!

May the *"floodgates of heaven"* open for you as you pray this prayer!

.

12145884R00066

Made in the USA
Lexington, KY
27 November 2011